Memorable Monologues for Actors

Over 40 Unique, Modern and Stunning Monologues
by Tara Meddaugh

For all the actors auditioning out there.
Break a leg!

Special thanks *to Mike Bouteneff, Ari Roth, David Pinner, Milan Stitt (RIP), Jacques Levy (RIP), Deborah Knuth, God, Matt Schatz, Kevin Snipes, Gabe Davis, Sallie Patrick, Geoff Hitch, Anya Martin, Laura Gross, Nick & Olga Bouteneff, Arlen & Roberta Meddaugh, Aimee DeShayes, Pilar Millhollen, Tivon Marcus, Ashley Sherman, Seth Fisher, Elizabeth DeRosa, Van Hansis, Jyoti Mittal, Sam George, Ben Pelteson, Jaclyn Fjestad, Danny Bernardy, Lexy Fridell, Carrie Flynn, Stephanie Clark, Kari White, Lilah Fisher, Dominic Hall, Pam Mulkern, Lynne Kuemmel, Kirby Fields, Jonathan Auxier, John Trevellini, Craig Weiner, Collin Acock, Erin Coulter, Katy Mixon*

TABLE OF CONTENTS

Stand-Alone Monologues

Ferret Envy/Jyoti..Dark Comedy (8)

Disappointing Hell/Van...............................Dark Comedy (10)

March in Line/Stephanie.............................Dark Comedy (12)

Tinsel for Christmas/Stan............................Dark Comedy (14)

Single Crutch/Ben...Comedy (16)

The Beanstalk/Jack...................................Comedy/Drama (18)

Purple Banana Nose/Danny....................................Drama (21)

Rising Fast/Elizabeth..Drama (23)

Crispy Leaves/Lexy...Drama (25)

Cutting Down the Tree/Kari....................................Drama (27)

Monologues from Plays

Free Space/Ricky..Comedy (30)

The Other Three Sisters/Mary 1.........................Comedy (31)

The Other Three Sisters/Mary 2...............Comedy/18th Century (33)

Free Space/Tabby....................................Comedy/Absurd (35)

Brush Them Fleas/Mrs. Hilton...............Comedy/Absurd (37)

Black & White & Red All Over/Georgia....Dark Comedy/Absurd (39)

Ring Around the Family/Carolyn...............Dark Comedy/Absurd (41)

The Last Two/Lily 1.......................................Dark Comedy (43)

The Last Two/Lily 2.......................................Dark Comedy (46)

The Last Two/Daisy 1.....................Dark Comedy/Drama (47)

The Last Two/Scruffy.....................Dark Comedy/Drama (47)

The Last Two/Daisy 2.....................Dark Comedy/Drama (51)

Seventeen Stitches/Rachel............Dark Comedy/Drama (54)

Free Space/Amelia 1......................Dark Comedy/Drama (56)

Free Space/Amelia 2......................Dark Comedy/Drama (59)

Free Space/Amelia 3...Drama (62)

Pinhole of Joy/Leah...Drama (64)

Pinhole of Joy/David 1...Drama (65)

Pinhole of Joy/David 2...Drama (66)

The Last Two/Daisy..Drama (67)

Brush Them Fleas/Stacy..Drama (68)

Ring Around the Family/Jessica.............................Drama (70)

Movements of the Wind/Pollen K-10...................Drama (71)

Blackened/Sandy 1..Drama (73)

Blackened/Sandy 2..Drama (74)

Seventeen Stitches/Peter...Drama (76)

Free to be John/Mae 1..Drama (78)

Free to be John/Mae 2..Drama (80)

Free to be John/Mae 3..Drama (81)

Free to be John/Mae 4..Drama (83)

Free to be John/John 1..Drama (84)

Free to be John/John 2..Drama (85)

Free to be John/Mae 5..Drama (86)

Free to be John/Mae 6..Drama (89)

Free to be John/Mae 7..Drama (91)

STAND-ALONE AUDITION MONOLOGUES

Stand-alone monologues are not excerpts from longer plays, but intended to work alone as audition pieces. While there are brief descriptions before each monologue, they are partially open-ended as to character, setting, situation. In most cases, they can be played by a male or female actor. The age-range is also fairly open, with many being possible from teen years to middle age. However, most monologues were written for actors in their 20s.

FERRET ENVY
*After murdering her friend's ferret, Jyoti,
wrought with guilt, tries to make* some form of
amends.

————————————

JYOTI

I know you think I murdered your ferret, but—hey, stop
crying. You're gonna make me cry too. And you (starts
crying)—know—happens—when—we—both—start—oh!
I'm doing it too now...(gaining composure) Okay. Okay.
What would Xena do?

Julia, your ferret ran away. He did. I know you don't want
to believe me, but I know this, because...well, I saw him.
And I was wearing my glasses, so I had 20/20. Or 20/30. I
need a new prescription. But I could still see it was Foozu,
and he was wearing the yellow rain slicker, not the winter
coat you tie dyed for him, so I think he was headed for
Seattle.

And, I don't think we should go after him, Julia. That
Payless box wasn't big enough; you always forgot to feed
him, and when you did, it was usually just pebbles and
sticks—and I really don't think ferrets can live on that.
Seattle has a lot more to offer Foozu. Food, drinks, warm
shelter, intellectual stimulation, perpetual contentment.
He deserves that, don't you think?

I, I know coming in and seeing me with the knife over
Foozu's box makes it look rather strange. But...Well...You
miss him, don't you?

          (pause)

You know...I could be your ferret. Don't dismiss it right
away. I'd be a good pet. I like to curl up in small places

and I don't mind rocks and sticks. You could knit me a winter coat, and you don't even have to tie dye it if you don't want to. That's okay with me. Is that okay with you?

I'm gonna just rinse this knife off and throw this little bag away, and then I'll curl up in my box. I found a new one— a size 11! I'll wait for you there and you can throw me a ball, okay?

Unless, you don't want me to be your ferret. You don't need to back away from me...Don't you want me here anymore? If I'm not here, who's going to sing to you? I know the entire soundtrack to Sleepless In—don't be scared—I'll—but I don't know where I'm supposed to go, Julia.

   (pause)

I could follow Foozu. I could—I could go to Seattle...I'll follow Foozu.

But Julia, when I go, you'll have to clean off the knife again—I won't be able to do it...I don't have a yellow slicker.

[11]

DISAPPOINTING HELL

*Van ends up in a physical altercation with his
soul.*

VAN

I wouldn't be here if I hadn't seen my soul tonight. I didn't
know it was my soul at first, but when it started talking to
me, when it started telling me how I was scared of being
hit by invisible cars, how I was only happy listening to
Simon and Garfunkel...well, it sounded so much like me.

So I go to it. I go to it and ask it, if it could tell me one
thing, just one thing about itself, about me, what would it
tell me. So it hesitates at first, you know, like it can't
decide what delicious secret to tell me. Then it sighs, as
much as a soul can. It sighs and sort of hiccups a little.
Like maybe it's overexcited. Or drunk or something. So
when it's done making these sounds, it stares at me with
its transparent eyes, and it says, in this tiny voice—the
voice a fawn might have, or a baby lamb. And it says, "If
you live through today, you'll get fired tomorrow. And
when you get another job, you'll get fired from that. And
when you find someone you love, that person will leave
you. And when you die, no one will care."

So what do you say? What do you say when your own soul
tells you you're a failure? And it looks pretty happy about
that too. Almost giddy. Like it's having fun telling you
you'll end up alone. So I start to wonder if it's really my
soul at all. If it's someone else's—like maybe my arch
nemesis or something, and it's telling me all this so I give
up hope. Stop fighting for the good side and my enemy
wins. By forfeit.

So I say the only thing I can think to say. And I do the only
thing I can think to do.

"I don't need you," I tell it.

(pause)

And then I squash it. And I kill it.

(pause)

And that's why I'm down here, I guess.

(pause)

I really thought it'd be a lot hotter.

MARCH IN LINE

Stephanie leads her stuffed animals in a serious mission.

STEPHANIE

I'm thrilled you all could make it tonight, gentlemen. I know I ask a lot of you, but I hope you all realize, I notice everything. Every tiny smile, every command obeyed, every sacrifice given. You're my men, aren't you? And tonight, you're going to prove it.

Now, I want you all to pick up your instruments and line up in—You! Stand up straight, please. I said, stand up! Would you like the whole town to see you in a wrinkled band uniform? Don't answer, just listen.

(pause)

Now, form that single line and reflect on your assignment tonight. Remember, you're more than simply clarinet players or baton twirlers. You have a mission, a purpose— and while you may not be here to witness the difference you make, know that I will. And that's really what matters most, now isn't it?
So all those people who said I didn't have a voice, who said no one would ever listen to me—those awful people, with their awful taunts in my head—"She called 'fire' and no one heard her!" "Have you noticed how the waiter never stops at her table?" "She can't even get a dog to lick her hand!"

Well, Awful People's Taunts! Look at me now. Listen to me now. I have all these gentlemen right here. Haven't I, gentlemen? Don't answer, just think! You're all prepared to march out that window, march out with flutes and

[14]

heads held high, and fall to your fated death...all for me. All for me.

Ready?

      (pause)

Oh, no! Mr. Teddy, your stuffing is seeping out again! I want you to look perfect when they all witness my power over you. I'll grab a needle. But the rest of you, begin marching.

      (pause)

Begin marching!

TINSEL FOR CHRISTMAS
After delivering a Christmas tree to his ex-girlfriend, Stan ends up bleeding in the hospital, and no one seems to notice him.

———————————

STAN

I think I'm next actually. I was here—well, I'll just wait then. It's just my arm is kinda bleeding right now and I was here before that woman with the twitch. But I'll just wait over here. Maybe you can't see me very well. Maybe I'll just wave my arms around like this. Is that better? Now you can see me real clear, right?

Well...I think I should stop waving my arms around. It's just my arm is dripping on things, well, the blood anyway is dripping. 'Cause it's Christmas, y'know, and my girlfriend wanted a real tree. But I have allergies. I sniffle a lot. I think it annoys people. Well, I can't help sniffling, y'know. I wish I would stop.

But I know my girlfriend's been real disappointed not having a pine tree for the past few Christmases—so I thought this year would be different. But I never used a chainsaw before. Lot harder to handle than it looks. And since my girlfriend decided to take a break from me this summer—I lived with her...in a house. You don't mind I'm dripping on the floor? I'll take my sock off. Here. I'll wrap it around my arm. That's smart thinking, right? I don't mean to mess up your nice floors. They're so yellow. That's nice.

But now that my girlfriend thinks I don't have any motivation 'cause I lost my job 'cause I couldn't keep up with my figures, well, now we don't live with each other. So I thought it'd be a good time to get her a real nice tree for Christmas since I won't be around to sniffle at it.

[16]

'Cause they said it's not in anyone's best interest for me to spend time with my girlfriend since she didn't like my calling on all my breaks at work to make sure she was okay and tell her I loved her. It's a dangerous world out there. I used to get a break every two hours. I've never been on salary yet.

Oops, the blood's soaking through my sock. Well, I have another one, I guess. But then, it's not so comfortable wearing shoes without socks. My girlfriend used to say my feet smelled like sour milk. I guess they do a little bit. So I'm not supposed to see her really, but giving her a Christmas tree I cut down by myself isn't so bad, right? Oh, I really think I should see a doctor soon. I'm kinda cold, y'know?

Well, I may not be seeing my girlfriend or anyone really on Christmas day, but at least I got her that tree. Left it on their porch. And that's why I have to see a doctor. Because she has good aim with that gun.
        (holds up arm)
As you can see.

I hope she decorates it with lots of tinsel.

SINGLE CRUTCH

After a bully steals Ben's crutch, he asks his friend to borrow one so he can make marching band auditions in time. Ben is a teenage student with one crutch.

———————————

BEN

I've been practicing my clarinet all morning and I really thought I was gonna get in this time. I know marching band is competitive, especially for the hockey team, but I had a good feeling about it all morning. Fifth time's a charm, my mom said.

Then that guy who wears all the jewelry stole my crutch.

My mom said it was okay for me to practice my song outside, since it wasn't raining and I was only playing marches. But he ran up to me from across the street. He was yelling something like, "shut the hell up!" or something. And he knocked my stand over and grabbed one of my crutches. I tried to run after him, but I'm not very fast on one crutch. I didn't let him get my clarinet though! I had to toss it under the picnic table, and I'm sure I broke the reed, but at least I saved it.

Anyway, now I have to sort of hop and walk to get anywhere. I don't think I can make it to the gym on time with only one crutch. And since you have that crutch you used in fourth grade when you were Tiny Tim, I was wondering if I could maybe borrow it. I know you want it to stay in mint condition, but I won't mess it up. I'd have to bend over a little, since it's a kiddie crutch, but my mom said I have a strong back. I don't mind.

Hey, you're the reason my leg is broken anyway. You're the one who told me to jump off the truck so Lisa would see and fall in love with me. But since the truck was going 30 miles an hour—and you weren't supposed to be going that fast—I just got this broken leg instead.

Fine, it wasn't all bad. The hospital did have HBO Plus. I saw Austen Powers two times in one day. But Lisa didn't fall in love with me and now I have to hop and walk. So I don't care if you don't want fingerprints on your Tiny Tim crutch. I think you owe me! This is my chance to get in the marching band and show Lisa I'm worth something. So give me your crutch or I'm gonna tell your mom!

THE BEANSTALK

*After climbing up a giant beanstalk for hours,
Jack is lost and anxious. He finally sees another
life, a black crow, and discusses his options for
getting off the beanstalk.*

———————————

JACK

Please don't poke my eyes out! Wait—don't leave! I
mean, unless that's what you were going to do, poke my
eyes out—were you? But otherwise, just, just stay. I—I—I
mean, you understand my worrying about that, right?
But—well, you don't seem like those birds. Right? And,
even if you are, I'm not like those girls. So. It's just—I
really am happy to see you. I'm getting a little, well,
maybe a little anxious. I don't know if you can tell, but, I'm
kind of a little bit stuck up here.

See, I didn't...really...think that I'd make it this far up. I
didn't really think it through at all. My mom keeps telling
me that's my problem, and I guess it is. I just...saw it, and
I've always been a bit of a climber, my mom said. When I
was nine months old, she found me sitting on top of the
brown cow in the barn one morning. I guess we all have
our strengths. I've never really considered myself afraid of
heights before, but, it's not really the climbing up that
scares me. It's the getting down, Black Crow. It seemed
so easy getting here—just put one foot on the branch—if
you can call it a branch. They sure don't seem like
branches now—looking down. Oh, and, I've tried going
down already. I put my foot on a branch, but it seems
slippery now. See? It's like the sludge at the bottom of
the pig trough. And you do not want be climbing down
from the clouds on pig sludge! I'm not a bright boy. They
all tell me that, but that is one thing I do know.

And see, that's why this is so, so, kind of tough to swallow. Maybe I was proving something. Maybe I was running away. I don't know. But I was doing something. You know? Climbing up something. Something that wasn't there before, but then suddenly was, and it made me feel powerful and strong and, and, smart. And I liked that feeling. So I kept on going, because the feeling kept on going. And, I'd never felt that way before. I mean, strong maybe, but—not smart.

But now I'm here. And I don't feel very smart. Because a smart person would know how to get down. I can't gain any footing on the sludge branch. I tried sliding down, but the few feet I did it, well, it hurts an awful lot, and I'm not even sure I wouldn't fly off of it and land down there in a broken bone pile. And, then everyone would just say, Well, that's Jack. He doesn't know how to climb down, poor slow boy. And I guess they'd be right. So.

       (pause)

The other thing I could do...and this probably would show I'm just as slow of a boy. Because it sure doesn't seem like a smart idea. But it's all I can think of to not kill myself falling.

       (pause)

See, I'm starting to hear voices. And not like voices in my head. I haven't turned silly yet. These are low voices. Really low. Booming voices, but not too loud yet. If you know what I mean. Like, a low rumble, sort of like a bull when he sees his mate. So the idea, Black Crow, is just to...keep climbing up. And maybe there's someone up there, one of the voices, who can help me, who can show me how to get down, or take me down. I'd be ok if someone else carried me down. I'd just ask them to do it at night, so no one in town would see. And I'd keep my eyes closed, so I'd remember it less. And then I could still

[21]

sort of feel a little powerful. A little smart. So see? I've
got it thought out now. At least a little bit. That's a step,
right? So. I guess maybe I'll see you up there. If that's
where you're going too.

(pause, starts going up)

It really doesn't feel like sludge when you're going up the
stalk.

PURPLE BANANA NOSE

*A mentally retarded man is being interrogated by
the police. He was present, although not
participating, at the time of the crime, but his
"friends" left him behind to face the authorities
alone.*

DANNY

(covers head in hands and shakes head)
Not s'posed to tell! Not s'posed to tell!
(uncovers head, looks up)
I tell but not use names. Okay? That's what Jimm—that's
what my best friend tell me to do. No names. 'Cause
we're best friends. My friends always save the cherry one
for me. They good friends. 'Cause I useta play by myself,
but now they play games wi' me. My friend teach me S-s-
s-sah-li-taire. Put black on red. Black on red. Black-on-
red. Blackonred.
(pause)
Why I gotta tell you 'bout the game we play? It our game!
My game wi' my friends!
(pause)
We gonna play Muppets, he tell me. You be Gonzo! He
tell me. GONZO!
(pause)
Gonzo got a purple banana nose. I like Gonzo. They tell
me be Gonzo 'cause Gonzo weird and stupid. Like me.
(laughing) They funny. My friends.
(pause)
We gonna do Muppet Caper. My friend Pe—my friend, he
play Kermit. And one play Piggy but he's a boy, not a girl.
(laughs) He's a boy, not a girl. (laughs) Boy-not-girl.
Boynotgirl. (laughs) They all silly. (laughs)
(pause)
I don't wanna tell you no more. You're not laughing. You
don't think my friends funny. (laughing) They make me

[23]

laugh. (stops laughing) But you make me cry. Why you
look like you so mad? Wanna go home. Don't wanna stay
here. You look so mad. Don't wanna talk.

>(pause)

Muppet Caper. They go inside, they play. Gonzo stays
outside and watches. Gonzo watches for the police.
When police come, Gonzo go inside and yell, "Over the
rainbow! Over the rainbow!" Then Gonzo stay there. Till
muppets grab him and pull him away—to safety! (claps)
Then muppets go back to J—my best friend's house and
eat poptarts—I get cherry with sprinkles—and cocoa.
(laughs) That s'posed to be Muppet Caper! Muppet
Caper! Muppet Caper!

>(pause)

But when police come and Gonzo go inside, no muppets
there. And it look bad inside. Gonzo look and look.
"Beaker! Fonzy! KERMIT!"

>(pause)

I forgot to say rainbow.

>(pause)

They gone.

>(pause)

But you there. With your gun. (laughs) But you didn't
wear blue hat then. I like your blue hat. And you take me
here and make me talk to you and tell you my game. Wi'
my friends.

>(pause)

They be here soon. They tell you. They tell you our game.
I didn't take nothing. I didn't hurt no one. I play game—
Muppet Caper. I'm Gonzo! Purple-banana-nose. "Over
the rainbow, Miss Piggy! Over the rainbow!"

RISING FAST

A girl confesses to her mother that during a
terrible flood, she lost her sister's baby.

ELIZABETH

I—I saw the baby, Mom, the baby, he...She calls me, Clara
calls me around noon and says the winds are getting bad
and water levels are rising. I'm sitting there, eating
popcorn, watching reruns of Ally McBeal on DVD—and the
whole town is evacuating! She asks if I can come to her
place, give them a ride to your house. So of course, I tell
her I'll pick them up. I don't even hesitate.

I walk outside and it's pouring, and I see the water rising
too. Rising fast. But I get in my car and start for her
house. The wipers can't keep up with rain, so I drive less
than 5 miles an hour. It takes me forty-five minutes, forty-
five minutes to drive one mile to her house. But I get
there. And I'm not even thinking about how we're going
to get out of town, how I'm going to get my car to move
again. I'm just so relieved to be with my sister, and the
baby.

But when I stop the car, when I crawl out the window and
look up at her house...her cozy ranch-style home...it's not
there. It's just...not there. I mean, there are pieces of it,
there are boards and there's the frame or whatever it's
called. But it's not a house anymore.

And I start screaming and running around—as fast as I can
through all that water—and I'm terrified because I can't
find them—then I hear a cry, a baby cry, and I see my little
nephew, sort of propped up in a piece of broken gutter,
between two boards, and I start toward him. He sees me
and I think he recognizes me! I'm racing, I'm moving as
fast as I can, but the winds are so strong and the water is

[25]

so deep. Then I hear this giant crash behind me, and I stop and turn around. That big oak has fallen on my car. It's crushed.

And when I turn back, when I turn back to see my nephew and grab him and bring him away with me...he's not there. He's not there anymore. Like the house.

I turned around, Mom. I turned around and I lost the baby. I lost Clara's baby.

CRISPY LEAVES

After a physical run-in with a florist, a young
woman visits her mother's grave, informing her
of a change she is making.

LEXY

Yes, the tulips are dead, Mother. But I didn't originally
plan that. Plan on giving you brown tulips. With crispy
leaves. I tried to refuse them, but...I'm just not good at
talking to florists.

But I know it's important to you—to have fresh flowers on
your grave. So this afternoon—when she—the florist—
when she brings out these dead ones, I try to explain. But
still be polite, like you taught me. So I say, "Ma'am, thank
you for the thought, but—" And I put my hand out, I
gesture, to sort of make my point. And I'm not done, but
that's all I get out, when she shoves them in my hand and
almost screams at me, "You're welcome!"

So the flowers are in my hands and she's looking at me,
grinning, like she expects money or something. And I'm
about to pay her, I'm about to pay her for four dead tulips
and leave—when something—I don't know, something ·
suddenly surges through me, through my veins—like I've
got new blood in me! Powerful blood! Strong blood that
people will listen to! Respect! So with my new blood
pumping through me, I grab the tulips with one hand and
this lady's neck with the other, and I shove those moldy
flowers all over her! I shove them in her ears, and her
mouth—since she's got it open, screaming—and just all
over her face! And it feels so good, Mother! It feels so
good...

Then I look back over at the brown tulips and I wonder if
they're all really dead? And I want them now. So I let go

[27]

of the woman and I cut off a little piece of blue ribbon from the counter, and I tie it around the flowers. And I come here. To you.

And I know you're used to getting fresh flowers every day, but I want you to know that I'm not coming back tomorrow. Or the next day either. Because it's a two hour bus-ride to get here and I have a job now [and I hate the bus.][1]!

So you can have these dead flowers, Mother. But I'm keeping this tulip. Because it still has a little green in its stem.

[I'll see you at Easter.]

---

[1] Dialogue in brackets may be omitted if desired.

[28]

CUTTING DOWN THE TREE

Kari cuts down a tree that has stood between herself and her lover. But the consequences have brought them together in an unexpected way.

KARI

I cut down that Maple tree tonight. I didn't want to—I didn't want to have to cut it myself, but, well, you know how it's been taunting me. How it's been standing there with its scraggly baby branches outstretching toward me as if it wanted to—trap me or scratch me or something.

And I've asked you to make it stop—I gave you a chance first. To make those branches more...I can't be expected to go to work every day when a Maple tree wants to steal my breath! And being an Administrative Assistant is the best thing that's ever happened to me—so if you expected me to give that up for the tree, you were wrong!

After all, you gave up quite a bit for the tree—and look where it's gotten you. That wasn't very smart, now was it?

I can still see you sitting against its trunk, basking in that awful shade—reading your stock prices, calling those girls, clipping coupons from the Sunday paper—well, who do you think picked up those Campbell Soup vouchers when they blew away in the breeze? I want to save 30 cents too, you know!

But you don't know, do you?

Well, now you will. We'll have a lot of time for each other now that Maple won't be blocking our sunlight.

I feel like you want me to apologize. To say I'm sorry for what I knew had to be done...Doing what's right or what's

[29]

hard—are they the same thing?—it's never come naturally to me, until now.

I don't think I knew you had drunk too much and were passed out under the tree when I cut it down. Look at your brown hand—it doesn't wiggle anymore.

But those branches do. Hm. I think they're trying to hug me now. I'll hug you later, Branches. For now, I must sit.

MONOLOGUES FROM PLAYS

A few inconsequential interjections have been cut from some monologues in order to make them unified.

Genre associations (dark comedy, drama, absurd) are intended to inform the reader of a general sense of the style of the excerpt. However, these genres may not apply to the entire play; a full length play may be a dark comedy, but the monologue excerpted may be a dramatic piece.

For more information on the complete plays or to find out how to receive a copy of a specific play, visit the playwright's website at www.tarameddaugh.com.

Comedy

FREE SPACE

Amelia spends her days under the watchful eye of her mother, doing the same nothing she has done for years. Yet when Bingo arrives at her local community center, a talking Bingo chip convinces Amelia that forming her own game is the way out of this life and away from her controlling mother. However, as her mother begins acting like a newly arrived sister, and the chip becomes increasingly dominating, Amelia discovers her new life is nothing as she imagined.

Setting: Ricky is a hardworking, kind and straight-forward young man at the local cannery. When Amelia comes to visit him, she confesses to a mistake her family has made. Ricky attempts to make her feel better about this.

RICKY

Mistakes happen though. To you and your mom, and it happened here at the cannery once—a lady came in a few months ago and said that she found a dog toenail in her can of corn! And that was not on the label. She was gonna sue us or something, but then the foreman gave her a free case full of canned corn and also some canned peas, because she said she really liked peas a lot better than corn anyway. I told her if she just got the canned peas instead of the corn in the first place, she wouldn'ta had this problem and it woulda saved her some time that morning. But she just kinda smiled and said everything always works out for the best. And I think it did for her, because she was beamin' as she packed her car up with that case of cans, and I don't think she was thinkin' anything about that dog toenail at all anymore.

[32]

THE OTHER THREE SISTERS

*In juxtaposing times and places, Mary wrestles
with the presence of the man in her life, Watts.
The 18th Century Mary in London, based off of a
short story written by Jane Austen, must decide if
she will accept the hand of a man she hates to
spite her unwed neighbors, or allow her younger
sisters to receive this honor before she. The 20th
Century Mary in Queens must decide if she will
allow her husband, who has returned after years
of a mysterious absence, to enter her life once
more and be forgiven. While the time and place
have changed over 200 years, the issues of
appearance, family, money, and love remain the
same.*

Setting: 20th Century Mary has recently seen her husband
who has been gone for years. She speaks with her two
younger sisters about this experience. They cannot
believe that he did not return with a good reason for his
absence; he told Mary he was gone because he had fallen
asleep. Mary explains his reasoning and her frustration.

———————————

MARY

I asked him— 'course, I asked him. I said, "What the hell
kinda reason is that?" And he said, "I was tired. I was
tired and I had to sleep. It wasn't you, darling. Why would
you think it was you? We were married four days, what
could you do wrong?" So I asked him then why he didn't
tell me then—five years ago—why he didn't tell me then
he was gonna leave and then he tells me, he goes, "I didn't
plan on being away five years, sweetheart. It just
happened that way. I was just going down to the creek to
sleep." So then my Rip Van Winkle says next thing he
knows it's now and he comes back to see his wife and here
he is, and that's fine and all, but what the hell kind of

[33]

reason is that? I mean, really, what the hell? The butcher thinks he joined the army in Kuwait, my neighbor thinks he ran off with a girl from Wisconsin and the old woman who sits behind me in church thinks he's on a fishing expedition with National Geographic. I got a dozen more interesting places my husband has been--any one of them I'm satisfied with. But to have left me because he wanted to sleep? Angela's husband left her because he couldn't stand how loudly she always breathed. Debbie's left her to join that tobacco farming cult in Chicago. Even Jilian's husband left her at least for an exotic dancer. What would the ladies say if I told them my husband left me because he was tired? I mean, really, what the hell?

THE OTHER THREE SISTERS

*In juxtaposing times and places, Mary wrestles
with the presence of the man in her life, Watts.
The 18th Century Mary in London, based off of a
short story written by Jane Austen, must decide if
she will accept the hand of a man she hates to
spite her unwed neighbors, or allow her younger
sisters to receive this honor before she. The 20th
Century Mary in Queens must decide if she will
allow her husband, who has returned after years
of a mysterious absence, to enter her life once
more and be forgiven. While the time and place
have changed over 200 years, the issues of
appearance, family, money, and love remain the
same.*

Setting: 18th Century Mary has finally agreed to marry the
large, ugly, boring Mr. Watts. While she does not love him,
she would hate for his offer to go to her younger sisters
and see one of them married before she. Additionally, her
neighbors have not received an offer of marriage, and she
looks forward to holding this over them. While she dreads
a life with Mr. Watts, she looks forward to the riches and
society gatherings a marriage affords. She reminds him of
what he owes to her, and becomes increasingly excited
and demanding as she imagines her life with him.

MARY

Remember the pinmoney—two hundred a year! And
remember I am to have a new carriage hung as high as the
Duttons', and blue spotted with silver. And I shall expect a
new saddle horse, a suit of fine lace, and an infinite
number of the most valuable jewels. Diamonds such as
never were seen! And pearls, rubies, emeralds and beads
out of number. You must set up your phaeton which must
be cream colored with a wreath of silver flowers round it.

[35]

You must buy four of the finest Bays in the kingdom and you must drive me in it every day. This is not all. You must entirely new furnish your house after my taste. You must hire two more footmen to attend me, two women to wait on me, must always do just as I please and make a very good husband. You must build me an elegant greenhouse and stock it with plants. You must let me spend every Winter in Bath, every Spring in town, every Summer in taking some tour, and every Autumn at a watering place, and if we are at home the rest of the year, you must do nothing but give balls and masquerades. You must build a room on purpose and a theatre to act plays in. The first play we have shall be "Which is the Man," and I will do Lady Bell Bloomer. You ask what you are to expect in return for all of this? In return, why...you may expect to have me pleased!

FREE SPACE

*Amelia spends her days under the watchful eye
of her mother, doing the same nothing she has
done for years. Yet when Bingo arrives at her
local community center, a talking Bingo chip
convinces Amelia that forming her own game is
the way out of this life and away from her
controlling mother. However, as her mother
begins acting like a newly arrived sister, and the
chip becomes increasingly dominating, Amelia
discovers her new life is nothing as she imagined.*

Setting: Bertha, Amelia's mother, has woken up in the
morning saying she is now Amelia's newly arrived sister,
"Tabby." "Tabby" is an energetic, bubbly, assertive girl
with big plans for their relationship. Since Amelia keeps
referring to "Tabby" as "Mom," "Tabby" tries to make
Amelia feel better about her lack of memory for names.

TABBY (BERTHA)

Don't be embarrassed. Mom said you need a little help
socially. Hey, I've even done it before too. I went to this
Christmas tree lighting ceremony once—in a really big city
far far away from here. And I was standing there by
myself—I wasn't by myself, but I just didn't know anyone
else around me. Well, when they lit the tree, I noticed the
lights—all lit together—looked rather like a Jelly Bean
Snow Globe. So I said to the man next to me, "Have you
noticed how the lights—all lit together—look rather like a
Jelly Bean Snow Globe?" Well, he certainly hadn't noticed,
but he said he did see a resemblance now. And he put out
his right hand and said, "My name is Chuck." Well, we
talked for the next minute or so and I realized I'd
completely forgotten his name. So I just asked, and maybe
you should try this with me, I just asked, "I'm sorry, can
you tell me your name again?" And he just said, "Sure. It's

[37]

Chuck." I still forgot a few more times, but I just kept asking and he just kept telling me it was Chuck. And finally I remembered. Why don't you try?

BRUSH THEM FLEAS

*When Mr. Boland's dog is murdered at an
upscale grooming salon called Brush Them Fleas,
each eclectic individual present becomes a
suspect.*

Mrs. Hilton, a high-end customer at the salon, has just
witnessed a fight between two of the employees at Brush
Them Fleas. After one employee suddenly changes her
story of what happened, Mrs. Hilton steps in to impart her
wisdom. They are in a waiting room.

———————————

MRS. HILTON

Lying isn't good, dear. I once lied I was a senior citizen
when I wasn't—I wanted to get a ten percent discount at
Heebies—you know, the donut store. I went right up to
the register and spoke in my elderlyist voice I could find,
"I'd like a half a dozen jelly filled donuts with my senior
citizen discount, please." Oh, I fooled that girl alright. She
just rung it up with no questions asked. Well, she asked if I
wanted coffee, but you see, I get real bad bathroom
problems when I drink coffee, if you know what I mean. I
see you smiling, you know what I mean. So, I told her no
thank you, of course. I was tempted to get it anyway, just
because I could get it ten percent off, and that's not a
savings you see every day. Most days you can find
something for ten percent off, but not every day can you
find everything ten percent off. Which is what is was like
at Heebies. On Tuesdays--senior citizen's day--it's twenty
percent. But I was there on a Monday or maybe a
Wednesday, but it wasn't a Tuesday. Well, I got that
discount alright. She brought me my donuts and I only
paid $2.13 for those jelly filled d-nuts. But you know, the
next day, I found ten more grey hairs and seven more
wrinkle lines. All of a sudden, they were just there. Nature
said if I was going to try to reap the benefits of an old

[39]

woman, I may as well look like one. So if you don't want
to look like an old woman, you better stop lying!

BLACK AND WHITE AND RED ALL OVER

When a man is charged with a mission to find his
wife a new heart, he sets into motion a series of
unusual events, resulting in four strangers being
left in his bathroom. One individual has a will,
one has a makeup bag, one doesn't know his
name, and one has a gun—and no one has any
idea why anyone else is there...

Scene: Georgia is speaking to a young man and woman
who have just met in this encounter. The couple is in the
bathtub, shower curtain pulled so Georgia cannot see
them, but they are presumably making love, as they both
have admitted they are young and attractive, and this
should be the natural course of events. Georgia is a makeup artist, and older, believing she has much wisdom to
impart.

———————————

GEORGIA

What a lovely time to meet. Well, I'll offer you just a bit of
advice, if I may. I should think you ought to purchase a
dog before you have children, considering that is the
patriotic thing to do. And I'm sure you'll find many
advantages to this purchase, as well. My husband and I
bought a dog and named him Granddad after my
granddad. Granddad had a terrible habit of running into
the street and he was hit by a car one day and died, right
before my eyes. Then we bought another dog and named
him Granddad after our previous dog that died. Granddad
had a nasty compulsion of chasing cars and so one day a
car ran Granddad right over and he died, just simply died.
After that we bought another dog and named him Mugger.
But Mugger was just like the rest and got hit by a car and
died. I was, naturally, quite disappointed, this having been
our third dog that died and all. Then as I walked to
Mugger's body, a neighbor stopped me and told me I

[41]

ought to keep my dogs on a leash and perhaps they wouldn't run into the road and die quite so often. Well, I thought this was an absolutely brilliant idea and so did my husband. Why, it was just perfectly horrific picking up Mugger's body from the street. I said to my husband right then, "Husband, this is just perfectly horrific picking up Mugger's body from the street. If we ever own children, we must heed our neighbor's advice and keep them on a leash." And so we did, and so we have ever since and we've never had to pick up their bodies from the street. I would suggest that you two purchase a dog first.

RING AROUND THE FAMILY
*At a bridal shower for her future sister-in-law,
Stephanie must decide if she will reveal a dark
secret, releasing this new family member from a
terrifying bond, but risking her own freedom and
happiness.*

Setting: In an effort to keep Stephanie from revealing a
secret to Jessica, a story is concocted that Carolyn's
husband has no hand. Carolyn runs with this idea and
further elaborates the lie to Jessica. Carolyn is a
somewhat nervous and excitable woman with a great deal
of energy. They are in the living room.

———————

CAROLYN

Yes, it's quite fun when Halloween comes around. He's
always a pirate. Arrrr!
　　　　(*she points her finger like a hook and smiles*)
Sometimes he wears the hook anyway, to parties, on
special dates, and the holidays, of course. I got him a new
hook for his birthday last year. Oh, he obsesses over his
hooks. Green, platinum, orange, gold, silver. Why it's
absolutely wonderful to have a husband who has only a
hook for a hand. Would you like to know how he lost his
hand? It was an accident. A fly accident. He was swatting
flies and—you see, our house is next to a farm with lots of
horses, so there are always a lot of flies on our property.
Well, since we're not horses, we don't swat them away
from each other with our tails. We're too "advanced" for
that, right, Jessica? So we use fly swatters and Max also
got those fly paper things that you hang on the ceiling and
stuff? Well, so one day, Max was hanging up the fly paper
sticky stuff and he was on a chair. But you see, my
grandmother gave me this chair, and she was never really
a handy woman around the house, so it was kind of
wobbly. You know how chairs get like that, right? So as

[43]

Max was standing on the chair to put the paper up, I called to him from the kitchen. I said to him, I said, "Max, maybe you could stick that paper on better, huh?" Well, you know how men don't like it when you try to interfere with—uh—those manly sorts of things, so Max turned to me and said, um, "You do it yourself then, woman!" He called me "woman." And then he fell and landed on a huge knife that I was using to cut our carrots with, and well, the gruesome details aren't important really. The point is, he has no hand and we just love that.

THE LAST TWO

When Daisy, a dog who likes wearing pretty dresses, disappears in a dangerous city, Scruffy, a loyal guard dog, must leave the comfort of all that is familiar in order to rescue his friend.

Scene: Lily, an old fashioned woman who stands on ceremony, has been preparing for a New Year's Eve dinner with her ex-husband and his dog, Daisy. Lily's dog, Scruffy, remains underfoot as she speaks to him about the coming dinner party. They are in their living room.

————————————

LILY

Away from the pie! Away from the pie, Scruffy!
      (shoes him away)
Oh, for goodness sake! Your slobber is all over the graham cracker crust! What am I going to serve for dessert now, Scruffy? I can't very well serve strawberry rhubarb pie with dog slobber crust, now can I?
      (thinks for a moment)
Well...now...I suppose I did brush your teeth this morning.
      (looks in Scruffy's mouth)
Doesn't seem to be any additional decay since then. You've only licked a crust, after all. You haven't licked yourself, have you?
      (SCRUFFY shakes his head)
Good then. Well, I suppose it doesn't have to be ruined. But you must stay away from it now! Do you understand me? No more pie until I say you may.
      (pause)
Oh, please. You don't need to look at me like that. I didn't hit you, did I? I didn't strangle your little neck or stomp on your toe with my pearly blue high heels, did I? I didn't. I simply reprimanded you in a loving—but firm—manner. So you can drop the eyes and go about your evening.
      (pause)

[45]

Please, Scruffy. I don't have time to console your moping.
Our guests will be here any moment. In fact, they're late
already. Figures. Half past seven and no one's here.
What time was the invitation for? Seven. That's right.
Seven o'clock. One might think they weren't even coming.
One might even think they were trying to throw a bottle of
baking soda and vinegar all over our unsuspecting faces,
mightn't one?

       (pause)

But not me. And certainly not you, Scruffy. No, we always
give the benefit of the doubt, don't we? Isn't that in our
naturally good dispositions? It's in mine anyhow. And
yours, when you're not sneaking around licking pie crusts,
or peeing on the white sofa bed—yes, I saw that last week,
I just didn't say anything because I felt sorry for you, but
now it's come out, so there you have it.

       (The door bell rings)

Oh! That must be them! Thirty minutes late—that's not
their charm. Are my wrinkles showing?

       (touches her face)

Not even my marionettes?

       (shakes her head)

I told that ex-husband of mine that our laughter would
only bring me ugliness in my later years. Of course, he
knew he'd hardly have to see me at that point, so what did
he care? Lap up my laughter, then leave me with the
aftermath wrinkles. Men are clever, Scruffy. Clever and
devious. Don't you forget that. No, I don't consider you a
man just because you have testicles. You're just a dog.
My darling little Scruffy.

       (rubs him behind the ears)

I love you so very much!

       (kisses him on the forehead)

My joie de vivre!

       (door bell rings again)

Well, I suppose I've kept them waiting long enough.

       (to door)

Coming!

       (to Scruffy)

You sit there. By the love seat. Put your head back, you know, how I like it. You look so handsome like that. Stay. Good boy.

(She opens the door)

THE LAST TWO
*When Daisy, a dog who likes wearing pretty
dresses, disappears in a dangerous city, Scruffy, a
loyal guard dog, must leave the comfort of all
that is familiar in order to rescue his friend.*

Scene: Since Daisy's disappearance, Scruffy, feeling
partially responsible, has been lethargic and depressed.
Today is his birthday and Lily, his old fashioned, but loving
owner, confronts him. They are in their living room.

LILY

My goodness, Scruffy! I didn't see you there. Can you
only move your paw? Do you want me to step on the rest
of you? Here now—fetch your favorite ball. That ought to
get you moving. Is this not your favorite? I thought it was
the blue one, but maybe it was the...Scruffy, do you not
want your cake then? I don't think you've even lifted your
head enough to see. Well, I guess that's that then. You
know what I'm going to say, don't you? It's here—the
end. That's right. You are closing in on your end, Scruffy.
Lying here like a plate of moldy jello, jiggling your way
around the house. The listless look in your eyes when you
stare out the window. Yes, I see that look. I thought
maybe you just needed sunglasses at first, but when that
didn't work, I knew it was listlessness.   You can ignore it,
but the facts are the facts. You're 18 years old today. And
you know what that means, don't you? Well, it's often the
day one becomes a man. The day you stand up and realize
you have strength you've never known before. That you
can lift a 25 pound bag of dog food. That you can sing the
baritone in choir. That you can protect the girl of...But for
dogs...Well, eighteen is awfully old for a dog. Especially
one of your size.

Dark Comedy/Drama

THE LAST TWO

When Daisy, a dog who likes wearing pretty dresses, disappears in a dangerous city, Scruffy, a loyal guard dog, must leave the comfort of all that is familiar in order to rescue his friend.

Scene: Daisy and Scruffy are celebrating the New Year with each other and their owners. After they've eaten and played games, Daisy confronts Scruffy about running away with her. They are alone in the living room.

———————————

DAISY

Look, Scruffy, tomorrow is the start of a new year. Do you know what that means? It either means another year of remembering one day at a time…or it means starting a new life. A new adventure.
    (pause)
With me.
    (pause)
I've already decided. The moment I saw that invitation with the fireworks. I knew this was my chance. There's no more liquid in the medicine cabinet, so this is it for me. I will not spend another night being told when to sleep because of the moon! Maybe I don't want to sleep at night. Maybe I don't want to sleep at all. I don't know. And that's the beauty of it! I don't know, Scruffy! But I'm gonna find out. What I'm good at, what my life is meant to be like. Maybe I'll become a soprano and sing in the opera! I love to howl! Maybe I'll dance for a king or paint a portrait. Who knows—I could do anything still, right? I'm young. There is more than fetching sticks, Scruffy. Now, I know you haven't been planning this, and I wasn't planning on asking you, so I can see how it's a bit of a shock. But now that I met you and you seem alright, I think we might make a good team. I can't guarantee I'll always stay with you. I'm the kind of dog that likes to

[49]

travel around with different packs, you see. I can tell that
about myself. But I like you. You're honest and you're
cute and sweet. And I'd like to show you some things. It
kills me to see a dog like you all caged up with that
mother. ..So what do you say? You wanna change your life
with me?

THE LAST TWO

When Daisy, a dog who likes wearing pretty dresses, disappears in a dangerous city, Scruffy, a loyal guard dog, must leave the comfort of all that is familiar in order to rescue his friend.

Scene: Since Daisy's disappearance, Scruffy, feeling partially responsible, has been lethargic and depressed. Today is his birthday and Lily, his owner, has confronted him about how his lack of activity may be a sign he is close to the end of his life. They are in their living room.

SCRUFFY

I didn't think I was at my end. Until you said it. But when you said it, it finally made it make sense. Everything. I mean, everything lately. How I feel. Why it takes me a few hours to fetch the paper in the morning now. I used to love the sight of the paper boy, tossing the rolled up news like a stick. I'd rush out to catch sight of him. The only other person we ever see on this island. Except for...except when Marcus and, and, Daisy...but I looked forward to the morning routine. But now. He arrives and my ears don't perk up. I know I'm supposed to go outside. Do something. I want to stay in, lying on the floor, but I make myself get up. I know it's my task. But when I get outside, I don't know where to go. I feel lost. I know I need to find something, and I search around, and then I see the paper and it clicks. This is what I'm supposed to find. This is why I'm outside. I pick it up and expect my feeling of loss to go away. My purpose is fulfilled now. It should be fulfilled. But nothing changes. I have what I went out to get, but it's not what I wanted to find. But I don't know what I wanted to find. And I come back inside and I only want to lie down on the floor and let you trip over me. But my birthday—that I'm getting old, for a dog,

[51]

that I'm at my end...this makes it clear. I'm searching for my end.

Dark Comedy/ Drama

THE LAST TWO

When Daisy, a dog who likes wearing pretty dresses, disappears in a dangerous city, Scruffy, a loyal guard dog, must leave the comfort of all that is familiar in order to rescue his friend.

Scene: Daisy, a dog, coming of age, has run away from home. She has swum through a lake to a dark and cold city. She knows no one, but upon her arrival in the city, she encounters someone and asks for help. We do not see or hear who she speaks to. Daisy is an energetic, brave girl, but is out of her element here. She is outside in a dark space.

———————————

DAISY

It's just, I'm cold. And wet. I don't have a jacket, as you can see. And it is winter after all. Even if we don't have snow. And my ears must be plugged from the swim because I can barely hear you, let alone see you.
(pause)
Well, you could show a little sympathy perhaps. Maybe give me a sweater. Or that scarf. I don't believe you just swam through a half iced-over lake to find your way here, did you?
(pause)
I'm not crazy. The fur helps, but it doesn't dry off instantly. I've tried to shake it off, but it won't, the coldness won't go away. So a little decency is what I'm asking for. You're all layered up. You can spare a layer, I'm sure.
(pause)
Hm? No, I'm not being demanding. I'm...okay. Maybe I haven't been as sweet as I generally am. Let's start over. Okay? I'm Daisy. I'm a beautiful puppy, all alone in the world, just looking for some fun. And a little bit of warmth.

[53]

          (pause, giggles a little back at the
          person)

I thought that was more your speed. As soon as I saw you, I thought, this is where the next phase of my journey begins. With this handsome dog here. You know you have that look about you. That look of someone who's been around. Who's seen the world and who the world has seen too—and mm, that's where I need to be...So can you spare a layer now?

          (pause)

Oh, okay. Well, sure I can wait a little. I mean, if we're going back to your place. But since you have so many, and I'm sure we'll have to walk a little, can't you—

          (pause)

Yes, I appreciate it. Having a house to go back to, but I'm just talking for now.

          (pause. DAISY forces a smile)

Okay. I'll wait. I'll be patient. I just don't see why you can't...

          (pause)

Oh, I've been around a little. But you know. I'm not a city pup. I'd like to be though. I mean, I think I'd like to be. Can you speak up?

          (pause)

No, I'm mostly sure. I just—

          (looks around)

I just don't remember it looking like this before. So dark, you know?

          (pause)

I know it's night time. But there's something else.

          (pause)

Well, I was only here for one night last time. If this is where I was. I'm not quite sure. Then I went back home. So, maybe nights change from day to day.

          (pause)

Hm. That's true. This time there is no end. That does make it...somehow different. Or, I guess, this is my end. The out of doors. And...I should be happy. I guess. And I am! I met you now, and you'll give me some warm clothes

[54]

and take me back to your place and give me a new life, right?

> (pause)

Good. And I'm really happy about that. It's just what I always wanted. Well, I don't know if I always wanted it, but...it's what I want now...or what I wanted...I just wish it weren't so dark and cold...

> (pause)

Oh, of course. Yes, let's move along. Let's see where you live. I love looking at dog's human houses. In fact, I just left a dog's human house. On an island. In a house in the woods. I just left there to come here and...

> (pause)

Thank you. I'm so glad I have you to take care of me. Or glad I have you to take care of. A dog needs both really, to be happy.

> (pause)

Maybe I do need to clear my head. You'd help me do that?

> (she walks along the street, following
> an entity)

When does the sun come out?

SEVENTEEN STITCHES

*Two teenagers meet in vortex-like space
between opposing lines of people. While Rachel
is simply passing the time before she returns to
her place in line, Peter has stepped out of his line
in protest. As the lines begin to "close in" on
them, he must make a life-altering decision by
choosing to continue forging his path in his
father's line, or join the allure of Rachel's line, the
line "of diamonds."*

Setting: Rachel and Peter have just run into each other
while waiting in their respective lines. Peter doesn't
recognize Rachel, but she remembers him, and even his
name. She explains how they knew each other years
earlier, in elementary school. Rachel is about 14.

RACHEL

Of course I remember the name of someone who saved
me. I was on the teeter totter with Becky Hill—she was
really big, remember? She was my age—maybe six, or
whatever age you are in first grade. I think she weighed
over a hundred pounds already. I weighed maybe 40, or
whatever you're supposed to weigh at that age. So maybe
Becky didn't like me because I stuttered when I read Dr.
Seuss, or she was jealous that I still wore kids' t-shirts or
maybe she didn't like me because I was just who she didn't
want to like—I don't know. But when I was way up high
and she was way down low, when her totter was touching
the pavement, she pointed out that my hair was falling
down. My dad put it in a ponytail every day—that's all he
could do. She kinda laughed when she told me, and I felt
embarrassed so I put my hands up to sorta smooth it back.
It was really windy that day. Then, when she was sure my
hands were off my totter, she grinned at me—I could see
she'd lost her front vampire tooth. And then she jumped

off the teeter totter. I toppled right over. I cracked my head open on the black top. I had to get seven stitches. Or maybe seventeen. I can't remember. But when I was on the ground, feeling the burning heat from the pavement scorching my face, you came over to me. You touched the crack on my head, then you went to Becky and hit her hard in the stomach.

FREE SPACE

*Amelia spends her days under the watchful eye
of her mother, doing the same nothing she has
done for years. Yet when Bingo arrives at her
local community center, a talking Bingo chip
convinces Amelia that forming her own game is
the way out of this life and away from her
controlling mother. However, as her mother
begins acting like a newly arrived sister, and the
chip becomes increasingly dominating, Amelia
discovers her new life is nothing as she imagined.*

Setting: Amelia, an odd but sincere girl of about 20, has
just lost her volunteer position working on Bingo night at
the community center. Before she left the center, she
stuck several chips in her pocket, but upon returning
home, her mother took them away from her. She is
defeated and lacking purpose in her life once more. Her
mother tells her to sleep on the floor of the living room, as
her bedroom is now occupied. Alone now, Amelia lies
down on her coat to sleep. Then she hears something.

———————————

AMELIA

What?

> (she looks around and sees no one is there.
> After a moment, she settles onto the floor once
> more. Again, she starts suddenly and sits up.)

Who's there?

> (she stands and looks around)

Who said that? Who's talking?

> (she walks around the room and looks under a
> piece of furniture. She stares at something and
> her eyes widen.)

You...

> (She pulls out a single bingo chip from under the
> furniture and holds it up)

[58]

She didn't get you…You're a lucky chip—she took all the others.

(pause)

So…what do you want from me?

(pause)

Just to listen? But…why me?

(pause)

You really think I'm that special? That pure?

(pause)

Yes, I think I understand Bingo more than them too. I'm glad you noticed. Some of them still think that if you're prettier or smarter or people like you more—that you have a better chance of winning…But you don't.

(pause)

Well, it's hard to remember really, what I did before Bingo. I know I just saw it last week, but I guess I didn't really do too much before it. I just…I stared out the window with my mother…but besides that….oh—I guess I used to look at the stars by myself sometimes. Is that doing something?

(pause)

Because if I squinted my eyes hard enough, I could see myself on one of those stars. And I'd wave down to myself from that star and think, "I look so tiny on that earth." And then I'd wave up at myself from earth and think, "I look so tiny on that star." Of course, I know I'd be dead if I were actually on a star…but, sometimes, I'd really like to be there. But my mom said I shouldn't think about things so far away from me. So…I stay here. Now that I don't have Bingo at the Center anymore.

(pause)

My own game? Oh, I don't know if I should start my own game. I'm really not that great talking to people and stuff.

(pause)

You'd help me?

(pause)

I don't know. Why would I even want to—

(pause)

Well, sure, I want people to notice me, but…

[59]

(pause, smiling)

You think so? Well...maybe this is my chance to shine in front of everyone!

(lies down on floor, next to chip)

And when the game is over, someone would win. But most people would lose. But that one person, that one extraordinary person, would be the luckiest one in the world.

(pause)

Well, I like talking to you too.

FREE SPACE

*Amelia spends her days under the watchful eye
of her mother, doing the same nothing she has
done for years. Yet when Bingo arrives at her
local community center, a talking Bingo chip
convinces Amelia that forming her own game is
the way out of this life and away from her
controlling mother. However, as her mother
begins acting like a newly arrived sister, and the
chip becomes increasingly dominating, Amelia
discovers her new life is nothing as she imagined.*

Setting: Amelia has just visited her only friend in town, a
local cannery worker named Ricky.   She told him her plans
to start her own bingo game, and Ricky is willing to help
her. She is developing stronger feelings for him and is
excited about the possibility of seeing him more. She is
alone, walking home from this visit. She speaks to the
bingo chip in her hand.

———————————

AMELIA

He wants to show me an albino frog! I—
            (pause)
Oh, you're right. I guess I don't know how to act in a place
like a pet shop. With Ricky. And around all those frogs. I
wouldn't want to hurt them, but sometimes I do things I
don't mean to. And Ricky said that's not my fault.
            (pause)
But I did step on a frog once and—I think I broke his paw.
Or his leg. But I didn't kill him, and I even took off the
Band-Aid I had on my own knee and put it on the frog's
little leg. I wish it'd had a picture on it. Maybe a picture of
a mouse. Or a 'possum. He would have looked cute with a
'possum Band-Aid on him. But it was just a brown one.
Plain. So then I sort of—pointed him toward the road and
gave him a little push, to help him get started on his

[61]

way...And I knew even as I pushed him, I was directing him toward that road. And I don't know why I did that, because I knew he was going to get hit by a car. Maybe I wanted to see if the Band-Aid would save him, if he'd escape from under a car...But he didn't...maybe he escaped from something else though...

(looks down at chip)

No, I wouldn't! I wouldn't do that at the pet shop! I don't want to push any more frogs in that direction. I'll just go with Ricky and he can help me—

(pause)

Well, what's wrong with Ricky?

(pause)

He's not distracting me. I know we didn't talk about the Bingo game the whole time I was there, but that doesn't mean—

(pause)

I know I can talk to you too, but I like him. He's nice and he—oh! Maybe he'll want to look at the stars with me too! I can tell him all about our galaxy!

(pause)

Well, he might want to know.

(pause)

He might be curious!

(pause)

But I want to show him the stars!

(pause)

You can't—don't say such a horrible thing! You can't touch him! You're just a chip!

(shakes chip)

You're just—

(the chip falls from her hand suddenly, as though it jumped from her grasp. She follows it)

No—wait, don't leave! I'm sorry! I can still run the game—don't take that away from me! You chose me, remember? And I chose to hear you.

(She crumples to the floor next to the chip and the "two" are silent for a beat)

[62]

Okay. I won't go to the pet shop until after the game. This is more important now...Just don't leave me yet, okay? I just—let's just go home and make some posters.

FREE SPACE

Amelia spends her days under the watchful eye of her mother, doing the same nothing she has done for years. Yet when Bingo arrives at her local community center, a talking Bingo chip convinces Amelia that forming her own game is the way out of this life and away from her controlling mother. However, as her mother begins acting like a newly arrived sister, and the chip becomes increasingly dominating, Amelia discovers her new life is nothing as she imagined.

Setting: Amelia has managed to set up her own bingo game at the warehouse of the local cannery. Her mother has attended, much to Amelia's dismay. The game has spun wildly out of control, but it leads Amelia to finally confront her mother about the disappearance of her sister.

––––––––––––––––

AMELIA

But that day it was sunny and Tabby had on a pink t-shirt, and she went to the back of the house, and she pulled out that old rusted red wagon you would never get rid of— And she tossed some rope in the wagon, then she picked up one of those cinder blocks that was lying around since Dad built the house, and she put that in the wagon too. And I was there and I asked if she'd pull me in the wagon, if I could come with her, but she told me I was too little to come. I said, little was good in a wagon, but she said today it wasn't, and to go inside. And I didn't know where she was going—I didn't know what she was doing! How could I know, Mom? I was too young to know! So she pulled that little wagon behind her and she walked down the hill...and by the side of the road...and through that path with all the blue dragonflies that led to the river—the

[64]

same path we would always take on those days when it was hot. And no one ever saw her! Or if they did, they didn't stop her. They didn't ask why she was taking a 50 pound cinder block for a wagon ride. And when I told you, when I told you—when I tried to tell you—you didn't listen. You were glad she was gone because the screaming had finally stopped and you told me to play outside! And when she met the river, she must have walked in, and just kept walking, and walking, and walking, and even if she had wanted to swim—she had tied that cinder block to her ankles so tightly—it pulled her down, and she sunk and she sunk and she sunk...!

　　　　(pause)

She killed herself, Mom! She killed herself because she couldn't stand—this!

　　　　(pause)

She's not coming back!

PINHOLE OF JOY

As Leah's desire and obsession for human hair grows increasingly demanding, her husband must decide how far he is willing to go to satisfy his wife.

Setting: Leah and David have been married for years, but her personality has recently taken a sharp change. She is paranoid and fears her loving husband is trying to kill her or leave her. They are in their kitchen.

LEAH

You have a criminal sense of humor, David. You always have. When you hit our television, you laughed. When you hit the dog, you laughed. You hit the dog so badly she bled and bled all night. I saw her drinking her own blood— Because of course, you offered her no water. Just left her to wallow in her blood. The poor thing couldn't move because you'd broken all her ribs. You think I'm creating a story, but I remember it, David. I can see it happening. I can smell the iron of poor Flopsy's blood. She whimpered and pleaded with her eyes. But you just hit her again. I think you kicked her too. She choked on her blood and you laughed at the red bubbles coming from her nose and mouth. You laughed like you always do because you like to see others in pain and dying. And you take pride in being the one hurting them and killing them, and laughing at their bubbles of blood. You like that, don't you?

PINHOLE OF JOY

*As Leah's desire and obsession for human hair
grows increasingly demanding, her husband
must decide how far he is willing to go to satisfy
his wife.*

Setting: David is a strong kind man, who has given up his
high powered job to work at a gas station, so that he can
have more time to spend with his ill wife. David and Leah
have friends over to visit, and in recounting stories from
their day, David shares his.   They are in their kitchen.

――――――――――――――

DAVID

A woman in a beige Volvo station wagon came in this
afternoon and threatened to sue us. This morning she
decided to commit suicide—from the exhaust fumes in her
car. After a few minutes, she changed her mind—I guess
she figured living wasn't worse than dying after all. So she
ran inside and cried for two hours. This is what she told us
anyway. Two hours later she remembered her car was still
on, went outside and saw her one-year-old baby dead in
the backseat. She claims she didn't know he was still in
there. So the first thing she did was drive her baby to our
station and yell she was suing us for killing her baby. She
was thrusting him in our faces. He was wearing little
brown baby suspenders.

PINHOLE OF JOY

As Leah's desire and obsession for human hair grows increasingly demanding, her husband must decide how far he is willing to go to satisfy his wife.

Setting: David and his wife, Leah, are slowly dancing. While their marriage was once blissful, Leah is now paranoid, sick, and her former personality is almost non-existent. David still loves Leah with all his heart and misses their closeness. This is a rare moment when his wife allows him to express affection toward her and he savors this. They are in their kitchen.

———————————

DAVID

The first time we ever danced, you asked me. I wouldn't have had the courage to ask the most beautiful girl at the wedding. You were so intimidating to me and my friends. Thomas had already asked you and you told him no, and to go ask Gwen by the seafood platter.
        (he smiles)
He was so sure he could get any girl in the room. That's why you told him no, isn't it? And then you asked me. You walked right over to where I was standing—I was showing some kid a card trick—I don't do magic anymore, but then I used to always carry a deck of cards with me. And you grabbed the cards from my hands, gave them to the kid—and this was a special marked deck of cards too, Leah, not the dollar kind you can buy at any store. You grabbed my hand and said, "Let's dance." Maybe you asked me out of pity then, to make a point to Thomas. But—that's okay. You have given me the best twenty years of my life. And you don't pity me anymore. Do you, Leah?

THE LAST TWO

When Daisy, a dog who likes wearing pretty dresses, disappears in a dangerous city, Scruffy, a loyal guard dog, must leave the comfort of all that is familiar in order to rescue his friend.

Scene: After leaving home, Daisy has been living in a seedy city. She makes a living performing on stage, working for a faceless and controlling man. She looks at herself in the mirror and imagines she is speaking to a customer. She is alone in her dressing room.

DAISY

Well, hello there. Beautiful weather outside, isn't it? Lush and warm. Almost...hot. Lush and hot. So hot I had to tear up my old dress to allow my hot body to breathe...You see? The hem used to be down here, past my thighs, past my calves, past my ankles...but I tore it, I cut it, up to here. This is much better, no? My legs get sticky in this hot hot weather. Feel. You feel that sweat? I'm so hot. Aren't you impressed that I cut this dress myself? It used to have a collar, a tight collar that made my neck feel as if it were being squeezed so tightly. I almost couldn't breathe. But then I cut it, see? All the way down to here...so my skin could feel the air against it. So I could feel the air against my skin. Doesn't this feel cool now?

(she holds one of her hands with the other and places it on her chest)

I can breathe. Can you imagine that I took my old long constricting dress that made me feel almost like, well, almost like dying, and turned it into this piece of wonder? I've changed it so much...no one would even recognize it. I'm glad you think I'm beautiful.

[69]

BRUSH THEM FLEAS
When Mr. Boland's dog is murdered at an
upscale grooming salon called Brush Them Fleas,
each eclectic individual present becomes a
suspect.

Setting: Stacy, a shy assistant at the salon, winds up in a
room alone with a reserved customer, Mr. Boland. After
some awkward conversation, in an effort to prove she
does know a few things, Stacy explains her passion to him.
They are in a waiting room.

———————————

STACY

I guess, um, I know about plants. I took a Botany class at
the community college and I started planting my own little
garden. I'm not too big on pretty flowers—I guess I don't
think they're that pretty. Well, some of them are. But
they frighten me. Flowers always mean something. They
mean 'I'm sorry' or 'I love you'...Or you died. I do like
dandelions though. They don't mean anything. No one
cares about dandelions. They're a pain, and they make
your hands turn brown, and they don't smell or even look
that pretty. But I like them. Because if you get enough of
them, you have to squint your eyes to look at them—
they're so bright. And no one gives dandelions to another
person so they don't have any value. And when they get
old, they don't just wither away; they get grey hair like us
and then fall apart all over the grass and the air. But I
don't even care that much about dandelions. I like them,
but I don't care about them. I really care about carrots
and potatoes. I like planting them because no one sees
them. Most people don't even know what's hidden under
the ground. It's like—a different reality, but it's the same
world. You know what I mean? And no one takes pride in
carrots or potatoes. Now tomatoes—people care about
them. People show off their tomato gardens, but no one

[70]

says, 'come over and see my carrot garden.' And when I pluck the carrots out, no one really cares. But I do. I have almost fifteen books on raising carrots and different things to make with them. I know a lot about carrots.

RING AROUND THE FAMILY

At a bridal shower for her future sister-in-law, Stephanie must decide if she will reveal a dark secret, releasing this new family member from a terrifying bond, but risking her own freedom and happiness.

Setting: Jessica and her future mother-in-law, Elisabeth, are partners playing the game, "Toilet Paper Bride," at the bridal shower. As Elisabeth turns toilet paper into a gown on Jessica, they speak about their dreams. Jessica reveals she has always had the pipe dream of being a singer. She is a strong young woman, raised mostly in foster homes. They are in the living room.

JESSICA

Yeah, I used to sing all the time as a kid. It was the one thing no one could take away from me, y'know? No matter where I was or who was with me, I always had my songs. So I would sing in my bedroom or the bathroom or under a tree or on a bus. Sometimes I would even sing without using my voice. Does that sound silly? That was because some of the people I stayed with didn't want to hear me. My voice was like a paper cut in the eye to them. They hated it. I think it reminded them that I had a soul. But they couldn't make me stop. They tried. They could beat me or slap me or—touch me. They could try to rip out my soul and replace it with one of their used dead souls, but they couldn't ever really reach it. I kept my songs buried so far under my soul that even if they got the soul, they couldn't get my songs. What kind of person would want to take a little girl's song?

MOVEMENTS OF THE WIND

*As the wind sweeps through a garden, the
inhabitants (vegetables, flowers, pollen) must
confront not only the dangerous elements of
Mother Nature, but also the dangerous elements
of their own nature. Through sacrifice and
friendship, they must survive their trials and
come to populate another generation.*

Setting: Two pollens are the last remaining pieces to stay
on a wilting flower. All others have jumped into the great
unknown, presumably finding a luscious young flower on
which to create a new home. Pollen V-6 has been scared
to leave, so Pollen K-10, an older pollen who has trained all
others in how to make this treacherous jump to safety, has
stayed to convince the young pollen to leave the doomed
flower. Yet try after try, Pollen V-6 cannot make the jump.
She finally asks K-10 where he received the encouraging
statistics on the rate of success for pollen jumps. After
much hesitation, Pollen K-10, finally admits the truth.
They are on a flower.

————————————

POLLEN K-10

The statistics aren't real. I made them up.
(brief pause)
I tried to get information from the flies, but they're too
fickle. They forget what I've asked them to do almost
immediately after they leave, and they don't remember
me when they return. The friendlier bees tried to help,
but then, even the most honorable ones told me upfront
there was a conflict of interest. The birds don't care. The
Talls don't understand us. There was nowhere for me to
get the statistics.
(pause)

But...the statistics are true. Pollens survive the ride so much more than they used to, because they believe they can. They believe they're prepared, and they believe the pollens before them who took the training were prepared. And they really are prepared, Pollen V-6. And so they believe they will make it....And I believe we will make it.

BLACKENED

When Sandy, a new employee at a weight loss camp for children, discovers a dark secret about the facility, she decides to take matters into her own hands.

Setting: Sandy is in a dark room, presumably a prison. Her former employer of the weight loss camp, Angel, has come to visit her. Angel has classified Sandy as "below average," and Sandy's moral compass has been tested and confused. Angel had given Sandy an odd picture, which she now treasures.

SANDY

Hey! I put the picture up you gave me! I can't put it on the wall, since we can't have nails, but I just set it on the floor and let it rest against the wall. Sometimes I think it soaks up words and colors and stuff from the wall though. There's not glass to protect it from soaking up that stuff— cause we can't have glass in here neither. Even without the glass though, it still shines brightly and sort of reflects things like it did have glass on it. Sometimes I don't like what it reflects though. Oh, it's not my reflection I don't like—it's all that other stuff that it soaks up from being in here. It soaks it up and sometimes reflects it out. I wish it had real glass so it would block all that stuff from getting into my picture you gave me.
> (pause)

It looks real nice there on the floor, Miss Angel.

BLACKENED

When Sandy, a new employee at a weight loss camp for children, discovers a dark secret about the facility, she decides to take matters into her own hands.

Setting: Sandy is in a dark room, presumably, a prison. In an effort to save children from her immoral boss's weight loss tactics, she has committed a horrific act of violence against Angel, her boss. She is haunted by this, although she has yet to come to terms with her actions. She has been seeing a mute Woman who appears in her cell from time to time and speaks to her now. Sandy looks at a letter.

SANDY

Why are you here again? I can't deal with you today!
Where is Miss Angel? What'd you do with her? Tell me!
Why are you here by yourself? I need to talk to Miss
Angel! My mama wrote me. I have to tell her that. She
didn't think she ever would, but she did. I knew Mama
would write. I'm her daughter. We have a bond. Nothing
can break that. I said nothing can break that! You don't
believe me? How would you know? You think you're so
removed from this all. You're in it just as much as anyone!
You should see that by now! If anyone is removed, it's
Miss Angel and she ain't smug to me. She's loving and
caring and always will be. She loves me more than my
mama does, I think.
          (pause)
I have let my mama down. Me being in her life hurts her.
My mama wrote how she cries every time she gets a letter
from me. Here, look at this!
               (holds her wrinkled paper at her. WOMAN does
               not touch it)

[76]

See how she says that! She says, "Your words are those of an innocent child, yet you have admitted beyond a doubt your guilt. How you can write of television shows and games when your heart has been so...

(pause)

Blackened, I cannot know. I can't bear to read your letters. I did not raise you this way. Please do not write to me, Sandy, until you are ready to express your remorse. Show me that you still have a conscience, Sandy. Show me that you still know what is right and wrong."

(pause)

And I do have a conscience. Sometimes it gets lost, but it never leaves me. Where's Miss Angel? I admit that my thoughts and my feelings have gotten confused, but I did it to help humanity. My mama doesn't realize that. But I did it to protect all those kids. She wasn't treating them right. If you see how that camp is run, you'd agree with me. All those other people there were blinded to it. But I was not. So I stopped her! But I saved those kids. How can those kids be hurt at camp when now there's no one to run the camp? Don't look at me like that! Don't do that! I know what they say—but I'm not blackened! I thought about it. I thought about it afterwards and I think about it now! Kimberly saw me—she saw how I was thinking. I do have feelings too!

[77]

SEVENTEEN STITCHES

*Two teenagers meet in vortex-like space
between opposing lines of people. While Rachel
is simply passing the time before she returns to
her place in line, Peter has stepped out of his line
in protest. As the lines begin to "close in" on
them, he must make a life-altering decision by
choosing to continue forging his path in his
father's line, or join the allure of Rachel's line, the
line "of diamonds."*

Setting: Rachel and Peter are sharing cake while they wait
between their lines. Rachel has been waiting with her
father in her line, but Peter has abandoned his line and his
father. Rachel cannot imagine how he could leave his own
father, and Peter explains his bitterness.

PETER

One summer my father gave me a bike. I rode it
everywhere—for five days. I was so happy to be able to
finally get away from things and people and . . . A bike is
fast for a kid, y'know? Then this kid down the street, Jeff
Oakland, saw me with it and said he wanted it. He was a
lot bigger than me, maybe 2 years older. He had garden
clippers from his mom's greenhouse and that day, he
came at me with them. I put the kickstand down and told
him to leave me alone. I was right outside my parents'
house, so I figured nothing could happen to me. I was
safe, right? But he kept coming closer with the garden
clippers and barking at me to get off the bike. When I
didn't, he grabbed my right leg and held it while he dug
the clippers into my leg. The blood got all over the right
pedal and on the lightning decals my dad put on it. But I
wouldn't get off the bike. When he went to my left leg
with the clippers, I started screaming. I yelled that my dad
was gonna come out, so he better leave me alone. But

when my dad did come out, when he finally came out, he didn't do anything to Jeff at all. He just pulled me off the bike, stared at my leg and told Jeff to take the bike and leave. As my dad was carrying me away, I could see Jeff, just standing there, like he was waiting to get in trouble or something. My dad just yelled over his shoulder, "Take it." He gave Jeff my bike.

(pause)

My dad said if Jeff acted like that to get a bike, he probably had worse problems than I ever would, and it wasn't worth fighting over. But my dad couldn't afford another bike for me. And after that, I wasn't able to get away from things anymore. Until now. He should have made Jeff hurt. He should have been there for me when I needed him.

FREE TO BE JOHN

*When Mae falls for John, a powerful man of God
imprisoned by her uncle, she must sacrifice
everything to prove her love for him.*

Setting: After years of admiring the famed and powerful
John and his teachings from a distance, Mae meets him for
the first time. Her uncle, the king, whom she lives with,
has had him imprisoned, and she visits him in his cell,
bringing him fine food from the king's table. Given her
relationship to the man who imprisoned him, John doubts
her good intentions. Mae is awe-struck to be near John,
but she defends her actions. She is about 18 years old,
energetic, sincere.

———————————————

MAE

I...I...came here today because...I wanted to give you better
food than what you've been given. I wanted to give you
better company than you've had. I wanted to...make you
feel...better...to tell you that you have a friend in the court.
You are right. My uncle is weak, and many women have
exploited that. And my mother is cruel. She uses people,
uses men, uses me. She doesn't care who she hurts or
how much she hurts anyone. And I want you to believe
me, and there's no real reason why you should, other
than, I'm just, I'm just telling you now with my words and
maybe you can sense more than my words, but...but
believe me that I am not like that. I am sincere and, and I
think you're, I think you're a very amazing man...and, and
after all these years, I just, I just, I really wanted to meet
you.
     (pause)
But I've stayed too long. I knew it was crazy for me to be
here in the first place. I'm being a silly girl. I never wanted
to be a silly girl—I hate watching silly girls. Please, John—
oh, is it wrong to call you that? Can I call you John?

[80]

       (JOHN nods)
Thank you...John...
       (they lock eyes)
Please, forgive me. I'm embarrassed. And I'm leaving.
       (gathers food)
I never even asked if you wanted to talk to me. I can see
you don't want me to return again. I'm sorry.

FREE TO BE JOHN

*When Mae falls for John, a powerful man of God
imprisoned by her uncle, she must sacrifice
everything to prove her love for him.*

Setting: Mae has just left her first encounter with the
famous and revered, John. While he was skeptical of her
intentions, since her family has had him imprisoned, he
does invite her to return to his cell again, with fresh greens
for his nourishment. This gives her hope. She speaks out
in narration.   She is about 18 years old, full of life, sincere.

MAE

I am exhilarated from our first meeting, short as it is. It
amazes me how in one moment, hearing him say my
name, that one syllable, can take my fear of rejection and
replace it with beautiful blood coursing, or, fleeing through
my body. Fleeing at the speed of...of...wild horses. I am
scared, but I am buzzing. My mind is racing like it never
has before. He's a prisoner. Yes. He's been jailed by my
uncle, because of my mother. He could hate me. Maybe
he does hate me. I wouldn't blame him if he hated me.
But seeing him, talking to him, for the first time after all
these years...even when his words combat mine, I drink
them in like the sweetest wine. No, he is not as I have
imagined him. He would be a fool to draw me into his
arms the first time we meet. And I'm a fool to have
dreamed it. He is more than I imagined. My heart has
always loved him. But now my mind is able to justify that
love. I've met him. We've talked. And he wants to see
me again. The moment he asks for fresh greens and I walk
for five hours through the desert to the water's edge to
pick them until my hands are raw...I know that this is a
man I will do anything for.

FREE TO BE JOHN

*When Mae falls for John, a powerful man of God
imprisoned by her uncle, she must sacrifice
everything to prove her love for him.*

Setting: Mae has been regularly visiting the powerful and
revered, John, in prison. Each time she sees him, her
feelings for him grow stronger, although she does not
know if her love is returned. She speaks out in narration.
She is about 18 years old, energetic, sincere.

———————————

MAE

Times passes quickly with John. I see him every day. And
it is all I live for. It's wrong to say that. I know it even as I
think it. But I cannot help it. He is my fantasy. He is the
man I've seen from a distance for years. I have seen his
charisma. He has made Pharisees repent. He's made men
in the highest positions fall to their knees asking for grace.
He has baptized thousands of men who are desperate for
his blessing. And the women...the lines and lines of
women who turn to him for guidance, in love, some pure,
but many lusting for him. I don't fault them. I am one of
them. How could I not be one of them? He is tall, a head
higher than most men, his chest is broad and firm, his
arms are powerful. His face is brown, which I love, with
striking lines. His eyes are green, and it may sound trite,
but I really can see warmth in them. And confidence. He
is kind, but he knows that what he is doing, what he is
saying, is always right. Because there is inhuman power
behind his words, his actions. Even the king is in awe and
fear of him. How can I not lust after this man? This man
who is coveted by every woman I have ever seen...Even
those who hate him are drawn to him. And I finally get
him. To myself. He's not a fantasy anymore. He is real. In
front of me. How could he not be all I live for? I love
him...And yet, in my heart, way pushed down to the

[83]

bottom of it, where I would rather not see, I know, we are living in this fantasy...And I need to choose our reality, before someone else chooses for us.

FREE TO BE JOHN

When Mae falls for John, a powerful man of God
imprisoned by her uncle, she must sacrifice
everything to prove her love for him.

Setting: Mae has been visiting the powerful and revered,
John, imprisoned by her uncle. During this time, her
feelings of love for him have grown stronger, and she
proposes a plan for him to escape prison and run away
with her. John refuses this plan, holding onto an idea that
Jesus, his beloved friend, will save him. She is about 18
years old, passionate, sincere. They are in John's prison
cell.

———————————

MAE

But he hasn't saved you yet. And you can't wait for him
forever. Forever may come and you will be a dead old
man in prison. Or it won't come, and you'll be executed in
ten days. We don't know Herod's thoughts, my mother's
thoughts. How long they will keep you alive. I'm no
prophet, okay? But I am a girl and I do know people. And I
can tell you that if your Jesus is not here saving you right
now, and he really is a God, then he's not saving you
because he doesn't want to save you. And I don't know if
I'd want to make my whole life about someone who had
the chance to save me and didn't.
    (goes to leave)
I have the chance to save you. And I'll do everything I can
to save you. You have the chance to be saved. I'm not a
God, but I—I—I really do love you. And even if you don't
love me, yet, that should be worth something, John.
Shouldn't it? Think about it before you seal your destiny.

FREE TO BE JOHN

*When Mae falls for John, a powerful man of God
imprisoned by her uncle, she must sacrifice
everything to prove her love for him.*

Setting: John and Jesus, as boys, have undergone an
attack on John's childhood pet, a dove. When a pained
Jesus does not heal the dove to save its life, John says he
hates him. Jesus places his hand on John's shoulder, then,
as Adult John, he speaks out, in narration. John is in his
early 30s, a strikingly handsome and strong man.

JOHN

Jesus's touch was unlike any touch by any man. You could
feel energy in his touch. Movement. Like a liquid flowing
from his hand to your body. Feeding you, refreshing you.
He said it was not his time to heal. But anyone who'd ever
felt the power of his touch knew he could not help but
heal. It was in his veins, in his blood. And in that instant,
my pain, my anger, my misdirected hate, freed from my
heart and dissipated like a fine mist into the air. I could
never hate this man. He knew that. I knew it. There was
no one I could ever love more than my cousin. I would
follow him into the darkest of places. Except, as we knew
from my first birth celebration six months before his, he
was the one who would be following me.

FREE TO BE JOHN

*When Mae falls for John, a powerful man of God
imprisoned by her uncle, she must sacrifice
everything to prove her love for him.*

Setting: John and Jesus have just reconnected after years
apart, as John has been working in his ministry in the
wilderness. They are both thrilled to see each other and
share that connection, brotherhood, that only they share
with one another. They realize that it is now time for Jesus
to start his ministry, and Jesus asks John to baptize him.
John refuses. They are in a tent, near the Jordan River
where John baptizes. John is in his early 30s, a strikingly
handsome and strong man.

JOHN

You know why I live in the wilderness, even now?
            (pause)
So that I cannot be tempted by the slightest indulgence. I
don't eat bugs because I like the taste. I eat bugs because
I don't want to like the food I eat. I accept nothing from
anyone. It is a slippery slope, remember that, Jesus, when
you start accepting pleasures from others. And the
bottom of that slope is a pit with no humanly way out.
The wilderness—it offers nothing. And because of that,
everything. You can be tempted beyond your wildest
dreams in the wilderness. Because it takes everything
away from you and you start wanting and wanting. But
there comes a time when the wanting becomes such a
part of your existence, it weighs you down to the point of
exhaustion. And you will do anything to have that burden
taken from you. And that's when you see that it can be
taken from you. It has been taken from you: Don't want,
and you won't want.
            (pause)

If I baptize you, it will make me greater than you. I cannot be tempted with that.

FREE TO BE JOHN

*When Mae falls for John, a powerful man of God
imprisoned by her uncle, she must sacrifice
everything to prove her love for him.*

Setting: Mae recalls witnessing the love of her life, John,
baptize Jesus of Nazareth. Mae is awe struck by John, his
power, his striking appearance, his confidence. She loves
him already, even though she has yet to meet him. Mae is
a girl of about 18, passionate, sincere, strong. She speaks
out in narration.

MAE

I only see them together this one time. No one sees them
together after this. And no one has seen them together
before this, not as grown men. There are some who
believe John has never met Jesus when he places his hand
on his head. That he was just another man who came to
be baptized before John felt God's presence in this man.
But I see a look on John's face as he pushes Jesus's body
below the river's waters—I know this look. He is filled
with a love so intense, it bubbles out of him and spills into
the river itself. I see the love, traveling down the Jordan,
and when the crowds have left, I drink this love from the
cool water and think of John. This is not the love of
someone who has never seen a man before. This is the
love of someone who has seen this man in many ways, for
as long as he can remember. It is admiration, it is fear, it is
giving, it is pure. As John brings Jesus from out of the
water, it is as though Jesus's body continues to ascend, out
of the water, into the air, above us all, and we hear a voice
saying that this man is the son of God, and that this God, is
pleased with him. A moment later, John is handing Jesus a
cloth to dry himself with, and Jesus is surrounded by
hoards of people. I blink because I don't know if what I've
seen and heard has really happened. I'm not sure if it has.

[89]

But really, I don't care if it has. Jesus is not the man I am watching. John is standing there, dripping in water, his robe tight against his firm body. I want so badly to hand him a cloth. I want to wipe his brow, his cheeks, his neck. As Jesus turns to leave, he is followed by the crowd. Some of John's disciples follow him too. I'm filled with rage at this betrayal, but John is smiling. He actually looks peaceful. John is a strong man, but I can see immediately that when it comes to this other man, he is weak. And I know this kind of weakness. I know he can't protect himself from it. But at this point, he hasn't yet met me.

FREE TO BE JOHN

When Mae falls for John, a powerful man of God
imprisoned by her uncle, she must sacrifice
everything to prove her love for him.

Setting: John has asked Mae to meet his disciples, find
Jesus, and ensure he is "the one" the Jews have been
waiting for. There is a threat of imminent danger to the
imprisoned John, and before he passes up the opportunity
for Mae to save him, he must be certain who he is
suffering for. Mae travels with the disciples and meets
Jesus. They lead her through the busy streets. Mae is a
girl of about 18, passionate, sincere, strong. She speaks
out in narration.

MAE

As I walk with Jesus through the street, I see things that
make my heart stop. Lepers somehow finding their way in
the public to him, their skin turning to pureness in the
blink of an eye. Men whose legs have never worked—
they're walking after he blesses them. Blind men's eyes
being opened with Jesus' saliva—gross as it is, it works.
There's a woman sobbing by a coffin, saying her only son is
dead. Jesus stops and touches her shoulder. He says,
"Don't cry," then tells the man in the coffin to stand up
and walk. And he does. The healings are something my
mind cannot understand. Is this real in front of me? Or is
this part of Jesus' elaborate plan, a hoax of some sort? It
doesn't matter. Because the chaos that is created
anywhere he goes is undeniable. No wonder the officials
are frightened—I am frightened. There's a mob of
desperate hands and arms and legs, heads and hair—
screaming, shouting, pushing. I have no idea how we are
going to find even a moment of quietness between us. Is
this man ever alone? Could he ever be alone?

[91]

We keep walking and walking and walking. I think that the crowd will tire, but it doesn't. It just keeps on picking up more people, like a ball of dust collecting more dust as it rolls along. A few times, Jesus stops, standing taller than anyone else around, and preaches. The crowd is quiet. If they are not, he makes them be quiet. With his words. One word from him or one look in your eye, and you will be silent. He is not old, but he commands respect like that of the elders. Of the kings. I am terrified to be near him.

But we do find ourselves alone. We are inside a small tent—a friend of Jesus' owns it. Jesus has a house, a second house even, they say, in the high end of Capernaum and he's making residence in a tent. His disciples are now soldiers standing on all sides. I still hear the crowds. There is no way we could have peace. I wonder how he sleeps at night and I begin to understand why John lived in the wilderness...But in the noise, in the tent, we have our privacy.

FREE TO BE JOHN

When Mae falls for John, a powerful man of God
imprisoned by her uncle, she must sacrifice
everything to prove her love for him.

Setting: Mae has just visited Jesus for the first and only
time. She has been sent by John to find out whether Jesus
is "the one" the Jews have been waiting for. There is a
threat of imminent danger to the imprisoned John, and
before he passes up the opportunity for Mae to save him,
he must be certain who he is suffering for. Jesus's words
have been precise, loving, but firm. He points out how he
is fulfilling what "the one" was meant to fulfill, but he will
not give her assurance that he will save John from prison.
In fact, he seems content that he does not even need to
save John. Mae threatens to lie to John, in order to
convince him to leave with her, but Jesus says her heart
will lead her to tell John the truth. Now, as late as it, she
must return to John. They only have a few more hours in
which to carry out her plan to escape with him.   Mae is a
girl of about 18, passionate, sincere, strong. She speaks
out in narration.
*Note: This is a lengthy monologue.

MAE

He leaves me like this. I stay in the tent for a moment and
hear him, without missing a beat, start preaching to the
masses outside. He is confident, strong, his voice seems
somehow louder than before. He's asking the crowd
questions. "What did you go out to the desert to see? A
reed swaying in the wind? A man dressed in fine clothes?"
Jesus can be sarcastic in his speech—I've heard that
already. He is firm, he is harsh, but there's an underlying
gentleness to his words. I understand this gentleness
when he goes on to answer his own question—they went
to the desert to see a prophet, but not just a prophet.

[93]

More than a prophet. He's talking about John. My John...His John. And he says the words I feel in my heart, as well—"Among those born of women, there is no one greater than John." I hear a pause in his voice. I can't see Jesus, but I think he may be resisting tears. Does this man cry? But the disciples are pulling me out and ushering me through the tail end of the crowd. The sun is setting and we don't have much time. I wish I could listen to a few more words from Jesus. What else did he have to say about John that he needed to tell the crowd? I feel I should know this too. But now I need to see John. The day has already slipped by faster than I'd hoped it would.

The mood of our return walk has shifted. The sun is not brightly encouraging us in our quest. The moon is peaking through the clouds and the desert heat is fading. John's disciples are not talking as much this time. A few words, here and there, but mostly about the route we're taking. They're not joking. If anything, they're arguing. Apparently one keeps stepping on the other's heels. One thinks this is on purpose because, he says, the other always does this when he doesn't get his way in choosing the route, but he insists this is the safest route. We are not only talking about speed in our route now. We are talking about safety. I start to feel that even a girl in servant's attire should not be out like this.

But we do arrive at the palace, safely. Then find our way to the prison. The disciples will remain outside here all night, hidden, but within view. They will wait for my signal. I am nervous, giddy, as I approach John's cell. I have an answer, but I don't know what it means. I don't know what John will think it means. And I don't know what I'll tell him. But as I approach, a guard stops me. The guards never stop me—not now. They wouldn't stop me any more than they'd want to stop the flow of goods and money I get to them in return. But one does, stop me, before I even take a second step. He stands tall, does not look at me, but tells me the words I fear the most. "He is gone."

(pause)

I stand there, for a moment. I'm looking at him, to the left of him, the right of him. My legs have gone numb and apparently I start to sway, as the guard breaks from his stoic face and grabs my elbow to keep me up. "Your mother will be here any moment," he whispers in my ear. "She wants to talk to us before Herod's party. Don't be here when she arrives." I try to back up, but my feet won't move. "Where is he?" I ask. "John?" Hoping there is a place he has been moved to, hoping it is a real physical place. And not under the ground. "I don't know. Only the guards that took him know, and they haven't been back since." I mutter a thank you, wondering how I'm going to move, then suddenly, I find myself now standing by the disciples. I silently thank my feet for doing what the rest of me could not.

I am trying very hard not to lose it. I tell the disciples what's happened, what I've been told, but my voice is straining and I think I'm going to cry in front of these strong kind men whose biggest flaw is stepping on heels.

No one says anything for a moment. The disciples look down and for the first time, I can see a visible shift in their bodies. They look smaller. Softer. Then one stomps his foot hard on the ground. His body tenses and he looks around; he wants something to punch. The other wipes at his eye and mumbles something about the dust. I feel a stronger sense of panic taking over. If these men have lost hope, these men who seem to always know where to go, how to get there, and how to stay safe...then what hope do I have?

I guess I don't hide my feelings well, and maybe this is a good thing, because it seems to pull the disciples together.

[95]

The one who wants to punch elbows the other, maybe a bit harder than he needs to, and looks at me. He's clearly never loved a girl yet and he shakes his head. "Oh, no— she's gonna bawl. Stop her, would you? She's gonna use up all her fluid crying then get thirsty and ask for my water and we don't have time to go to the well for refills." This is the practical disciple, the one who knows the safest route. The other shrugs, like he doesn't know what to do either, but he pats my head and says, "There, there," which is a phrase I've never actually heard anyone say, so that, and the sheer awkwardness of his touch, actually make me smile a bit. He's pleased by this and beams at the other. "See? Works just like that on my old donkey too!"

There is no time for tears. No more moments of silence. We have to find out if John is alive. And if he is, where he is. I don't have many ideas to offer—it was enough that I had found where John was first placed. But his disciples know where to check. The "real" prison, they tell me. "If he's not there," one disciple pauses, "he's already with God."

So we continue on another journey into the night and my feet do as they're told. This real prison is not as close to the palace as where John has been staying. I mentally make notes of our path and estimate the time it takes so I can be sure to visit again, if I cannot bring John away right now. I will not allow my heart to think he could be dead.

When we finally arrive, it is late. I know Herod's party is probably only just beginning. I doubt my mother will care if I'm there or not, but Herod may notice. I wish I had told my maidservants something to say on my behalf. I had assumed after visiting John, that I would see them again and update them as needed, but the unexpected trip to Jesus changed those plans. Now I can only hope that they filled in the gaps and will not call anyone to look for me.

When I see the prison, my heart sinks. It is as dark and gloomy as you might imagine a prison to be. But my heart sinks the most because I don't recognize any of the guards. I have to recognize the guards or there is no way I will be allowed inside. The disciples assure me they are ready to storm the prison walls if need be, and as I am starting to consider their offer, two guards I know come outside the complex, and stand on our side of the gate.

I'm not sure exactly how to approach, and as I am foolishly saying this out loud, one disciple says, "Like this!" and shoves me out from the bushes into the gravel path leading to the prison. I want to turn around and yell at the disciple, but I know I can't give away where they're hiding. So I keep on walking, which seems to be my fate for this night. The guards are standing taller, seeing me now, but they don't take a step toward me yet. I'm no threat, so they are waiting.

I reach the gate and the two guards I know say something to the other guards. They nod, and without my having to mutter a single word, they open the gate and lead me in.

My heart, which has taken more than a beating tonight, leaps for joy because I know, I finally know, that my John is alive! I can stomach the sickening smell of vomit and blood and urine and any other bodily fluid that might be thrown about these walls, this dirt floor. I can ignore the screams, the wails, the bangs and whips I hear...because I am on my way to see my lord...at last, after this very very long day. I will see the man I live for.

As we approach John's cell, the guard tells me one more piece of news that helps my heart soar—"Herod said he won't kill him. He wants him to rot out his life in jail."

ABOUT THE PLAYWRIGHT

Tara is a graduate of Carnegie Mellon University's MFA program in Dramatic Writing. Her work has been presented by The Director's Company, Theatre One, Fusion Theatre, One Armed Man, Oracle Theatre, Inc, the Bobik Theatre  Ensemble, Woman Seeking…, the Acme Theatre Company, and various universities including Gardner-Webb and Colgate. Her plays have also showcased at the Artists of Tomorrow Festival in NYC, the Pittsburgh New Works Series and the Last Frontier Theatre Conference in Alaska. Serial monologues she wrote were performed for two years by the internationally recognized receptionist-robot, Valerie, and she toured in a Children's Theatre Troupe, which she wrote for, co-directed, and performed in. She has taught Playwriting and Screenwriting to students in High School, college and adult education programs. She has also led Creative Dramatics Workshops for children and teenagers in underserved areas throughout New York and New Jersey and has a background in social work. She is a recipient of the Shubert Fellowship in Dramatic Writing, the New Works for Young Women [Actors] Award and is a member of the Dramatist's Guild. Tara has written a children's book, a novel, and writes and records music in the chick-core rap band, Girl Crusade. She lives in Westchester County, NY, with her husband and dramatic toddler.

For more information about Tara Meddaugh or her work,
visit her website at: www.tarameddaugh.com.

Made in the USA
Lexington, KY
11 February 2018